How t
Stocks & Shares

(An idiot's guide)

By

Harry Scard

PLAYGROUND PUBLISHING

Published by:
PLAYGROUND PUBLISHING LTD

P.O. Box 125, Portsmouth
Hampshire PO1 4PP
Tel: 023 92 819162
Fax: 023 92 734814

© 2000 PLAYGROUND PUBLISHING LTD

ISBN: 09535987 4 8

Illustrations by Andy Jones
Limericks by Liz Garrad

Dedicated to all
you punters out there
who have yet to
make a profit with
stocks and shares.

A cross section of your average private investors waiting for their shares to go up

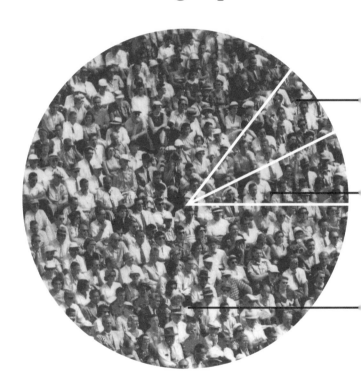

A simple categorisation of your average private investors, actively talking part in the stock market.

10% These are people who don't know anything.

10% These are people who know a little.

80% These are people who don't realise they don't know anything.

At the outset, you must be honest and decide which of the three categories you fall into.

How do YOU pick your shares?

Picking a winning horse is a doddle, compared to trying to pick a winner in the stock market. We are not talking long term here, because long term, even the dead will rise.

So lets examine the various ways you can pick your potential winner.

1   You can follow the tipsters, the brokers and the rampers.

2   You can study share movements, their highs and their lows.

3   You can study charts, the PE ratios and the comparable stocks.

4   You can study the companies, their directors, their products and their potential.

5   You can listen closely to the word in the city, and follow the big boys on the prowl.

... But none one of these, however, could guarantee with certainty a profit like our good old privatisation's did.

Why can't we just have more and more privatisation's. Surely there must be other things they could privatise.

Everything you ever wanted to know about privatisation's...

1   If with privatisation's, the government made billions, the private investors made a packet, the institutions, the stock brokers, the organisers, the television companies, the banks, the printers and the post office all benefited, ...then who were the actual losers?

2   Why didn't the government just send each member of the public £200, and just sell the shares to institutions. Wouldn't this have saved a lot of bother and expense.

3   Didn't anyone suspect why the number of heads per household soared when it came to counting the applications.

4   Were members of the public notified that the minimum requirements for applying for shares was that you had to be human and alive, and how many pets are still shareholders in these privatised companies.

Only one application per each member of the family...

What is the secret of success in the stock market?

What is the secret of success in the stock market?

You can research the stocks till you are blue in the face, you can read up the tip sheets and all other write-ups. You can study the charts, even pick the top 3 companies. That would still not guarantee you success.

The secret of success is knowing which crowd to follow, when to follow, when to stop, and how close you manage to get to the one right in front.

If you play everyday on the markets
if you study your shares in FT
if the Nikkei has frowned
on the cost of the pound
and the Dow Jones is down 10.3
If your GDM shares didn't rocket
if your profit's not making you proud
don't be a nutter and don't risk a flutter
be a sheep and just follow the crowd.

Just follow the crowd...

Of course you need money to deal in the stock market, ...

I'm lost and I'm broken and damaged

I'm homeless and out on the street

No bills have been paid

and my clothes are all frayed

And I haven't the money to eat

I'm down and I'm out and I'm dirty

I'm hungry and I don't mean to moan

But I just want to call my stockbroker

So have you got some change for the phone?

Should you share the intricate details of how you are doing in the stock market with your family?....

... Or should you keep them guessing...

A Share in the Boardroom

It is amazing how company directors always manage to buy and sell into their stock at the right time with pinpoint accuracy.

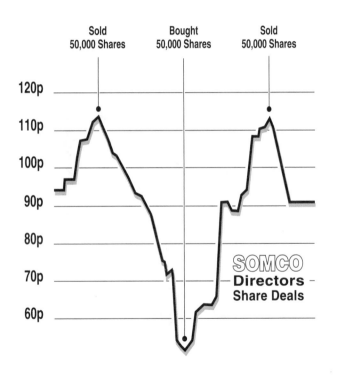

A Share in my portfolio

It is also amazing how I always manage to buy and sell at exactly the wrong time with pinpoint accuracy.
Still,..... it is comforting to know that if my buys were sells and my sells were buys, I would be doing just as well as the company directors.

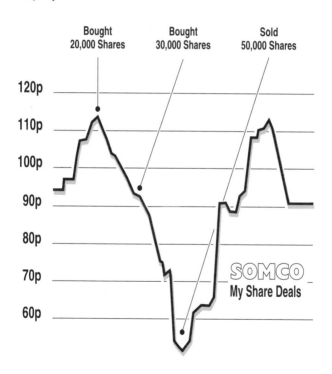

If you enjoy pain, ... sit and wait for that bounce.

I guess one of the most painful scenarios is when you buy for a quick killing, but the stock goes down. You stay put, because you are sure that the bounce is just around the corner. You wait and wait, and just watch the share going down and down to a place of no return.

I want to tell you a story my dears

I have been married for twenty eight years

My husband he loves me I know that he cares

And when we first married he bought lots of shares

he thought they would rocket it would happen quite soon

and that we could jet off on a nice honeymoon

Barbados, The Seychelles some place of renown

But the peak hasn't happened no they're still going down!!

19

How do you tell if your husband has lost money in the stock market.

he has become quite spiritual all of a sudden with _____ talk of death and the hereafter.

hands constantly reaching for weapons ofdestruction _____

sweat developing even in very cold conditions _____

eyes fixed in a state of shock _____

constant flow of tear from the corner of the eyes _____

mouth kept open, breathing becoming very random _____

body appears to be on auto pilot with little co ordination _____

knees shaking in fear of wife finding out _____

toes turned up from contraction of muscles from stress _____

To relieve stress after a huge loss, try alternative medicine

Advanced acupuncture sounds almost too good to be true.

Darling your losses have left me bereft
the furniture, carpets there's nothing left
I see you need help so it's all down to me
I know of this wonderful new therapy
It's advanced acupuncture it works on the brain
when you're tempted to deal well you'll simply refrain
the needles are thick to work better and quicker
the more that you lost well the nails become thicker
the bigger the losses you'll need so much more
Now keep still while I just nail your head to the floor.

After a huge loss, don't try fishing for sympathy.

I came home this evening quite humble
I fell down and confessed to the wife
That I'd lost everything on the markets
And I thought that I'd just take my life
She said darling - no really don't do it
There are much better ways you must see
She said things will turn out so much better
If you just leave the killing to me.

25

Watch out for those subtle signs of disapproval...

Could it be your choice of stock she disapproves of...?

My buddy he said buy some beef shares
it sounded the business to me
then my assets got frozen
'cause the product I'd chosen
was banned by the old EEC
So now I am broken and homeless
Bankrupt in debt to the teeth
I'm broken, bereft,
and the wife she has left
Do you think that she didn't like beef?

Keep subscribing to those tip sheets, ... they will eventually help you break even...

If there are enough of them, of course, and they are piled high enough to prevent you from getting to the phone.

Invest in a scheme to keep them away from the stock market..

Not doing so well?... Consult your wife, ...Women can be so practical.

My wife is an angel and I love her it's true
I was losing too much but she knew what to do
she said that my gambling was going nowhere
so she gagged me and tied me real tight to a chair
and now when I'm tempted or I just get that feeling
she hoists up my chair 'til I'm close to the ceiling
and just underneath just for both of our sakes
is a box of nastiest deadliest snakes
so far it has worked and it may be the cure
for although we're not rich yet at least we're not poor

They must care to go to all this trouble to protect us from getting hurt...

I woke up this morning
and I was surprised
I was totally plastered
and immobilised
my wife she was grinning
and said with some scorn
the bank statements come
and we're still overdrawn
so this is for us
and I'm not being mean
although you can't deal -
you can still watch the screen

Sometimes actions speak louder than words.

My wife she has got quite angry
and I really don't know why
she burnt my share tip leaflet
and then began to cry
she said I didn't care at all
and I should may be leave her
and then she broke my PC
with her very sharp meat cleaver
she pulled the phone out of the wall
she wrecked it anyway
if she doesn't like me dealing
then I wish she'd only say

Is this the turn around I've been dreaming of....?

I've had some great luck on the market this week
I bought some great stock and it started to peak
I followed the tipsters and my profit just soared
So I bought a bit more just to save being bored
I knew that for once that I'd just got it right
My stockbroker sold past my limit that night
the stock market's brought me just pleasure - no pain
Now should I buy a villa in Greece or in Spain
A yacht, a Ferrari with paint work to gleam
Oh there goes the alarm and it's all just a dream

37

I am not paranoid, ... I know they are out there watching me.

Of course I'm never paranoid
but what I say is true
If I sell stock it rockets
and I don't know what to do.
I buy it back and live in hope
of luxury and wealth
The screens all flash - it plummets
and it's damaging my health
So don't try to convince me
'cause I know the truth you see
The guys down at the stock exchange
have got it in for me.

Some of us can hide the psychological effects of losing in the stock market, ... some of us can't.

A note from someone who has lost it completely

My Stock Brokers lovely he's such a nice chap
If I don't have the money then he'll take the rap
The tipsters are caringand generous and kind
And they're always right I think you will find
The rampers, derampers they care for each other
With a love that you'd usually find from your mother
And let's not forget Market Makers So giving
Just trying to earn a clean honest living
I will not be told that they're dishonest thugs
Nurse can you come is it time for my drugs?

Of course I can think for myself, ... I think I'll follow the leader.

I have come to accept that the markets around the world take their lead from the US. ....And I even know why when America sneezes, we catch a cold. But..... there are still things that really make me wonder.

Have you ever wondered .....

1   Why the world markets always follow the US, with such pin point accuracy, as if to be operated by remote control.

2   Why the European markets bother to open a few hours before the US, if all that is done during those first few hours is to guess which way the Dow is going to go.

3   Why when the Dow or the Nasdaq fall, we follow with greater speed, but when they recover, we stay in the doldrums for so long recovering from the shock.

4   Why don't we simply close down the London Stock Exchange, and just wire our deals over to the US.

5   When WE will get the chance to play the leader, and let The US market follow ours?

The Technology Sector phenomenon

Didn't we know what was happening in the Technology sector. Didn't we realise the real quality of some of these Dot Com companies. Were we not warned of the bubble bursting? Then why oh why did we all lose so much money when it finally happened. ... and why did we deny it happening even when it was happening, and continued to lose during the decline?

Has the Technology Sector Crash left grudges against technology as a whole?

During a stroll along the high street, pop into the share shop for some really good bargains in the sale.

... and who knows you may run into someone who bought before the sales.

A sure way to double up .....

I was really in trouble with money

I was worried from dusk until dawn

I was really distressed

had my house repossessed

my account was well past overdrawn

My mate said, just try the stock market

You'll double up - it is a safe bet

Well he's right -

with no trouble the lot went double

Not the profit - no only the debt

**A sure way to
double up.
It really works, ...
I have tried it.**

The real crash victims, what a way to go

"Smedley!....Just nip down to the car park and move my Jag, will you!"

"You've no need to take it too hard Roger,....Your shares have gone back up again."

Everything you ever wanted to know about Stocks & Shares but were too embarrassed to ask.

- If tipsters really knew, how come they are not all millionaires, and why are they still scraping a living on a journalists salary.

- Why are penny shares so cheap.

- What would the FTSE do if Wall Street was closed for a week?

- With privatisations, why didn't the government just give £200 to every individual, and just sell the shares to institutions.

- What are market makers like at home, and do their kids' pocket monies fluctuate week to week.

- Why can't I make money on the stock market.

- Despite heavy losses everytime, why do I continue coming back for more?

- Wouldn't be easier if market makers just give us a bank account number for us to deposit money, instead of having to go through the laborious task of buying stock from them and then selling the stock back to them at a loss.

- If P/E ratio and Yield value are so important, how come they never affect the share price movements.

- Do market makers ever go bankrupt.

- Why are stock brokers so polite.

- Do stock brokers have a good laugh behind their clients backs

Everything you ever wanted to know about Stocks & Shares but were too embarrassed to ask.

• Do stock brokers have a good laugh behind their clients backs

Market Makers

The stock market evolves around a group of clever people called the market makers. They buy and sell shares, just like the rest of us; with a slight difference., that they dictate what price they buy and sell at. Without them, the market would be like the high street on Christmas day.

But who are these market makers? ... and if they really are as clever and cunning as we think they are, then why are they wasted in the stock market, and why are they not being used in espionage? or torture chambers?

Actually, I guess they are working in torture chambers, and you don't have to be with them to be tortured. It's all done on the internet, the phone and the television screen.

I am sure one could write volumes about this, elite camp, the tricks they play, and how to beat them at their own game. ...but for now it will suffice to say, don't let them scare you into making a mistake with their share price fixing, ...sometimes it could just be arbitrary, and without a reason.

A Market Maker in his lunch break...

The Market Makers' favourite tricks...

The market makers will use every trick in the book to trap you, so you must be prepared and familiarise yourself with the signs of these tricks. Remember the market makers thrives on volume. Volume based on being able to sell stock at its high and buy back at it low.

Let study how the run up of a stock would normally happen. Once the stock begins its climb, it attracts day traders and those in for a quick profit. The stock continues up until there is enough buying pressure. Once the buying runs out of steam, (that is usually when I come in and buy), then the decline begins building up momentum with more selling.

The more it goes down the more scared I become, until they reach a point at which all monkeys including me are shaken out of the tree. The market maker has filled his buy orders at very silly low prices, and he is ready for the next run.
It is only then that I wish I had held on, and bought more on the lows.

The tricks Market Makers play

One could write volumes on the scope of the tricks at
Market makers' disposal. I guess experience will eventually
arm you with the ability to watch out for the tell tale signs of
these tricks; meanwhile just be careful, and don't let them
play on your weakness...GREED, to trap you.

What they say and what they mean...

TIPSTERS

A company with huge
potential growth .... A one man band

Medium to long
term investment .... Who knows the shares may just go
up eventually

Medium to high risk................. For complete and utter idiots

The shares are oversold......... No one has any faith in this company

COMPANY DIRECTORS

Difficult market conditions........ We have lost it to the competition

We are well positioned
for recovery............................. Things couldn't get worse,
Another year like this and were out

Company requiring
cash injection........................... Banks want their money,...
on the verge of of bankruptcy

MARKET ANALYSTS

The economy is strong, ...
This is just a correction........... Here comes the big crash
followed by a long lasting bear market

Market is down because
of interest rate worries............. Don't know why this is down

Market is up as interest
rate worries recede .... Don't know why it is up

PRIVATE INVESTOR

My funds are all tied up .... All the shares I've bought are down,
and I cant sell until they bounce back

I am topping up....................... I am trying to reduce the average
based on the pathetically high price I
paid for the first lot

What they say and what they mean...

I am in the process of
transferring funds from
my other account....................................I am broke.

Diary of an idiot and his share dealing

Day 1   Having monitored the price movement of a particular share, and watched it go up for three consecutive days, he buys into the stock on account.

Day 2   The shares go down, but he stays calm, and says 'they'll bounce back up tomorrow'.
This is just a little profit taking for those who got in before the rise.

Day 3   The Dow and Nasdaq both down, the share loses another 10%. He says 'I've never seen these so low, so buys some more, trying to reduce his average price.

Day 4   The shares are down again, but he waits for the US market to open to consider his position. The US opens down, and his stock plummets to only 50% of their value.

Day 5   He waits and watches the price which stays put. He considers that this may be a breather before more declines, so he sells to settle the account. Late p.m., heavy buying and the stock rockets.

Diary of an idiot and his share dealing... a year later

Day 1   Having monitored the price movement of a particular share, and watched it go up for three consecutive days, he buys into the stock on account.

Day 2   The shares go down, but he stays calm, and says 'they'll bounce back up tomorrow'.
This is just a little profit taking for those who got in before the rise.

Day 3   The Dow and Nasdaq both down, the share loses another 10%. He says 'I've never seen these so low, so buys some more, trying to reduce his average price.

Day 4   The shares are down again, but he waits for the US market to open to consider his position.
The US opens down, and his stock plummets to only 50% of their value.

Day 5

He waits and watches the price which stays put. He considers that this may be a breather before more declines, so he sells to settle the account. Late p.m., heavy buying and the stock rockets.

I am not likely to make the same mistake again, ...Am I?

What is it about this statement which sends shivers down your spine. Specially when it is immediately followed by, "I know what I am doing this time". Then the inevitable happens,...and the same mistake is repeated again and again.

The evolution of the stock market punter...

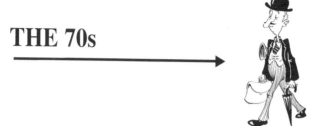

THE 70s

THE 80s

THE 90s

It is amazing what lengths some people go to, in order to make out how well they are doing in the stock market.

It is amazing what lengths some people go to, in order to conceal how well they are doing in the stock market.

Don't ever get emotionally attached to a share

Don't try to swim against the waves, don't be stubborn, and certainly don't get too attached to a share, or you'll be the one left holding the baby.

Do you have an emergency fund you can tap into...?

I admit, ... I am a loser...

It takes real character to be able to admit to your limitations, and accept that perhaps you were not cut out for certain tasks.

It is amazing how compulsive losers keep coming back for more. Having lost in all the deals they have ever made, they still believe that may be one day they will get lucky.

So they carry on, sometimes even going back to the basics, but to no avail. The road to success will ultimately rest with their ability to admit what they really are...

I've bought a book and it's really a steal
you can get rich real quick as you learn how to deal
It says you can learn if you just understand
so I thought it might give me the real upper hand
I didn't do well or get rich that quick
I just couldn't win so perhaps I'm just thick.

The Stock Market's Compulsive Losers Association.

The acceptance speech...

"I would like to thank everyone who helped me in getting where I am today. First of all I would like to thank my stock broker, whom I have know for many years. In fact we were like buddies, and it is only now that I realise he knew exactly what I was doing, but never said a word. The market makers who for some strange reason, seemed to always target my money personally. The tipsters who sounded as if they really knew what they were talking about. The rampers and derampers to whom I listened because I had faith in human nature. The company directors who always managed to delay those important announcements, right up to the moment immediately after I sold the shares. But most of all I would like to thank the Dow Jones and the Nasdaq for always managing to ruin everything, just when I was beginning to break even.

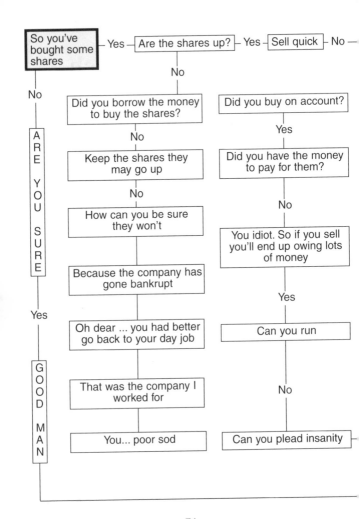

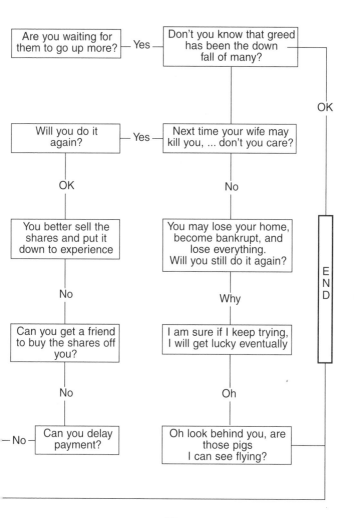

Keep a record of your financial position, and persevere towards your target

Year	No of Deals	Losses for that Year	Profit No Lies	Overall Balance
1987				
1988				
1989				
1990				
1991				
1992				
1993				
1994				
1995				
1996				
1997				
1998				
1999				
2000				
2001				
2002				
2003				
2004				
2005				
2006				
2007				
2008				
2009				
2010				£ 0.00

Keep a record of the non-financial cost of your stockmarket dealings

Year	Blood Pressure	Heart Beat	Broken Relationships	Years Aged	Cost of Stress relief remedies
1987					
1988					
1989					
1990					
1991					
1992					
1993					
1994					
1995					
1996					
1997					
1998					
1999					
2000					
2001					
2002					
2003					
2004					
2005					
2006					
2007					
2008					
2009					
2010					

To receive any of the products; simply fill in the order form opposite with your address on the back, and your cheque/postal order made payable to:
Playground Publishing Ltd, and send it to:

PLAYGROUND PUBLISHING LTD
PO BOX 125
PORTSMOUTH
HAMPSHIRE
PO1 4PP

If you wish your purchase to be sent directly to someone else(e.g.; Birthday, Christmas, Wedding, Valentines Gift), simply fill in their name and address in the order form, and enclose your cheque/postal order with your personal message or card, if desired.

We will be pleased to send your gift directly to your chosen recipient.

OTHER TITLES FROM
PLAYGROUND PUBLISHING LTD

copies   "Men Can Be Such Idiots,
But you gotta luv 'em"
ISBN: 0 9535987 0 5 ....£4.99

copies   "Women Can Be So Annoying,
But You gotta luv 'em"
ISBN: 0 9535987 1 3 ....£4.99

copies   "The Best of Notice Board Gems"
ISBN: 0 9535987 2 1 ....£3.99

copies   "100 Tips for the Frustrated Slimmer"
ISBN: 0 9535987 3..£1.99

copies   "How to Break Even with Stock & Shares"
ISBN: 0 9535987 4 .... £1.99

copies   "The Elderly back at Work"
ISBN: 0 9535987 5 ....£2.99

copies   "Kcalodisk"..£1.99

I have enclosed a cheque/postal order for: £ ....

made payable to:

PLAYGROUND PUBLISHING LTD

Name: ....

Address: ....

....

....

....

County: .... Post Code: ....

Fill in the coupon above and send it with your payment to:

PLAYGROUND PUBLISHING LTD

PO BOX 125

PORTSMOUTH

HAMPSHIRE

PO1 4PP

Postage FREE within the UK